ECCENTRIC AUSTRALIA
In search of Australian quirk

COME ON IN...
Before we *both*
STARVE!

In search of quirk

All countries have their own particular kind of quirk but Australia is a continent well known for its high quirk content.

Historically, in terms of European discovery and settlement, the first records of quirk were made by the early explorers. Australia's kangaroos stunned them; the Platypus, more than any other creature, caused intense curiosity. This now world-renowned creature was first recorded in 1799 by the British scientist Dr George Shaw. His initial reaction to the original specimen was that it was an elaborate hoax. He even took a pair of scissors to the pelt, expecting to find stitches attaching the bill to the skin!

Since then the nation's eccentric animals, characters and landscapes have attracted tourists, film-makers, photographers, writers and artists from all over the world – after all, no other continent has an Uluru, a Kookaburra or a Koala.

As a photographer I have long used the "pursuit of quirk" as a recreational activity while travelling from one place to the next. My eye is well trained in recognising the visual appeal of oddities in nature as photographic subjects and it is the out of the way places that have taken my fancy as places to prowl. The thrill of a quirky human discovery now brings me as much pleasure as finding and filming a new bird, frog or fish. In fact, as I grow older and maybe a little more cynical with the passage of time, the delightful peculiarities of human quirk become very hard to beat. I trust that you will enjoy sharing some of my quirky Australian discoveries.

Above and left: The Blue Heeler Hotel, Kynuna, north-west Queensland. **Right:** The Railway Hotel at Ravenswood in central Queensland.

The memories behind the mementos

In Australia's Outback, pub walls are often festooned with curios and unusual memorabilia, each piece of which comes with its own unique tale. The list of mementos has little consistency – coins, paper currency, number plates (although why anyone would carry a Kansas USA number plate deep into the Australian Outback beats me), prison leg irons, rabbit traps, bottles, stubby holders, pipes, undies, bras, shoes, animal skins, autographs and, quite commonly, polaroids of grinning travellers with one arm slung around a leather-faced "bushie" and the other raising a "coldie" to the local watering hole.

Outback pubs

Approximately 620 km from Darwin on the Stuart Highway is the famously cluttered Daly Waters Hotel. Dating back to 1893, this historic hotel is now one of the oldest buildings in the Northern Territory. The little town has a population of under fifty people, but the hotel has long been an important watering hole for stockmen droving cattle across the rugged Kimberley to Outback Queensland and is now a tourist attraction.

Curious and curiouser...

The Bridge Hotel at Jingellic on the River, New South Wales, is adorned with a variety of treasured bric-a-brac and memorabilia.

Animal oddities

Above: Koalas often assume entertaining, sprawled sleeping postures. **Right:** This Red-necked Wallaby really must do something about evicting its joey, which has grown almost too large to carry.
Opposite: A Common Wombat and a Red-necked Wallaby make an unlikely pair, but these two have been raised together since birth in a Tasmanian wildlife park, resulting in a strange friendship.

Australian animals are recognised worldwide for being uniquely odd. It's not just their bizarre appearance that delights the imagination, but also their postures, expressions and behaviour. People from all countries and cultures express amusement at Australia's seemingly thrown-together creatures.

Freaks of nature or fantastic, colourful creations?

Left to right: Orange-eyed Green Tree-frog;
Ghost Bat; Frilled Lizard; Short-beaked Echidna.

SLOW DOWN, you're in cassowary country...

Anywhere in Tropical North Queensland where there are Southern Cassowaries, signs warn motorists of the potential hazard posed by these delightful, giant flightless birds. On one sign, near Daintree National Park, a passing wag has mischievously added feet and a beak to a speed hump symbol along with the words "before" and "after". This inspired graffiti causes major traffic jams as tourists alight on the narrow winding road to take pictures.

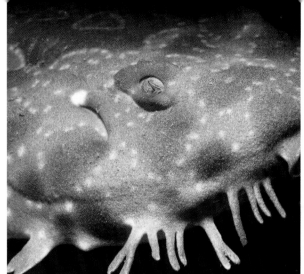

Fish, with their great diversity in colour and shape, have a strikingly original eccentricity.

Clockwise from top left: A fat-faced Star Gazer; this wobbegong has a face not even a mother could love; a beautiful blue-finned Butterfly Gurnard; and an Estuary Catfish.
Opposite: The Red Rock Cod has an impressively dangerous appearance.

Watcha lookin' at, fish face?

THE KING OF QUIRKY CREATURES

Leathery, large and lurking below the surface, the incredible Saltwater, or Estuarine, Crocodile occupies a position as the king of animal quirk. In north-eastern Arnhem Land, where these powerful predators are common, the "Saltie" is revered and its story is passed on to younger generations of the Gumatj people. For most travellers and locals, its fearsome reputation and gnarled, time-weathered appearance are awe-inspiring reminders of a prehistoric era.

Opposite page, left to right: A large "Saltie" makes short work of a wallaby; this elaborate Aboriginal artwork of a crocodile, Anyatjamarra, is in the Almutj Rock Art Gallery above Twin Falls in the Top End.
This page: A less intimidating, stylised "croc" in the Top End, Northern Territory.

Under normal circumstances feral donkeys are very shy. Rigid curiosity is their first response; the second is to bolt at an alarming speed. However, donkeys can be domesticated and have a history as pack animals and pets.

Making an *ass* of myself...

Australia is known for its eccentric animals, but one encounter with a particularly nasty creature has stuck in my memory. I was driving between Halls Creek and Fitzroy River when I came across a family of tourists. They were all running in circles around their car, followed by a large donkey. The donkey (left) had met humans before and obviously harboured some serious emotional issues for ... well ... donkey's years. I pulled over to offer my services, but as soon as I did so the donkey stopped its chase and zoned in on me – before long I was running around the car too! After the animal decided it couldn't catch me, it focused its attention on my car and set about gnawing off my windscreen wipers!

Left: The ass, another word for donkey, is depicted here in Oodnadatta with a less than endearing slogan.

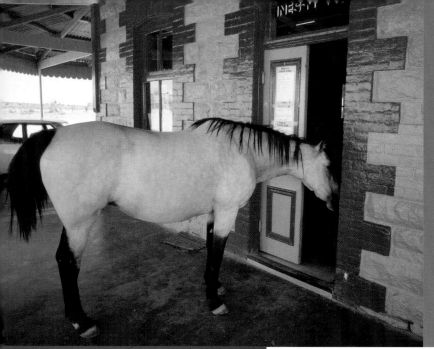

Horsing around...

From Phar Lap to the Goondiwindi Grey, two-horse bush races in Cape York to the Melbourne Cup, even to the horse that drank beer on hot days or the "small and weedy beast ... something like a race horse undersized" of A.B. "Banjo" Paterson's epic brumby-mustering poem *The Man from Snowy River* – Australian folklore is full of horse stories.

Above: A thirsty horse at the Silverton Hotel, New South Wales.
Left: This horse seems unperturbed by two letterbox horses sharing its paddock at Hungerford, central southern Queensland.
Bottom left: A two-horse race at Coen, Cape York, Queensland.
Opposite: The town of Goondiwindi, near the Queensland–New South Wales border, is famous for the racehorse Gunsynd. Nicknamed the "Goondiwindi Grey", the horse captured the hearts of race-goers by winning 29 times during the late 1960s and early 1970s.

Brian, from Yorketown in South Australia, built "Granny's Chariot" to give his ageing German Shepherd, known as Granny, a rest when he took his dogs into town. The chariot is drawn by the rest of the pack.

It's a dog's life

Top: "Big Bitch", the guard dog at the Tilpa pub, Darling River, western New South Wales.
Above: A ute-load of cattle dogs out on the town.

Lunatics

Thanks to its maniacal, grinning entrance, Luna Park is arguably one of Australia's most famous amusement parks, but its origins began in metropolitan New York's Coney Island in the late 1800s. Australia's first Luna Park was at St Kilda in 1912. In 1930, a second Luna Park opened at Glenelg, Adelaide, but was soon moved to Milsons Point, Sydney. Few amusement parks can claim to be located on a site with such an interesting history. Before Europeans colonised New South Wales, the bushland and foreshore around Milsons Point was home to the Cammeraygal Aboriginal people. After settlement the area became a popular picnic and entertainment spot from which, in 1789, Governor Phillip watched Aborigines perform traditional dances in return for goods and trinkets.

History on parade

The anecdotal history of Geelong, Victoria – from its Aboriginal inhabitants to more contemporary characters – is colourfully displayed by more than one hundred 2-metre high, brightly painted statues along the city's foreshore, providing a fascinating and fun chronicle of the city's rollicking past.

The vibrant bollards are the work of artist Jan Mitchell, who began the project in 1994. Over a period of nearly four years she and her team transformed old timbers and piles from the Yarra Street Pier, demolished in the 1980s, into remarkable works of art.

Australia's kangaroos, affectionately known as "Skippys", are so popular that international tourists expect to see them bounding down the streets of major cities. But, while it's unlikely they will see a real kangaroo in the centre of town, the many life-sized bronze sculptures of animals that adorn Australia's city streets – such as the kangaroos (left), pig (above) or swan (below) – seem as if they could spring to life at any moment.

Opposite, clockwise from far left: Errant kangaroos; a bush pig in the city is unlikely to cause this little fellow any harm, despite seeming about to knock him down; a bronze swan waddles past the Swan Bells Tower in Perth.
Right: Bronze sculptures provide climbing fun for enthusiastic youngsters.

When art becomes *quirk*

Contemporary graffiti is a trend that was spawned in New York during the early 1970s, but it only arrived in Australia, as with rap music, break dancing and hip-hop, around a decade later. It soon spread across Australia from city centres to the back streets of bush towns. The mural wall at Bondi (left) is an example of local councils being innovative enough to support the art. Some are also seeing the value of wall art as a major tourist attraction. Towns such as Ellison, on the Eyre Peninsula in South Australia, boast Australia's largest murals; others such as Sheffield, northern Tasmania, lay claim to the most.

Why hang your work on the walls of an art gallery when there are a million opportunities to scream very loudly at the masses?

Below: A wall mural decorates a building in Innisfail, north Queensland.

Above: Popular with backpackers and bohemians alike, Kombi vans decorated with colourful murals are a fairly common sight throughout Australia. This one is at Coogee, New South Wales. **Previous pages:** A mural adorns the exterior of a store at Streaky Bay, South Australia.

The twist of lemon

When it comes to quirk, the trick is to find that twist of lemon – something original, exciting or unique. This shot was taken in Quorn, a small town in the South Australian Outback. As I rounded a corner, my right eye saw a delightful, curtained window mural painted on the wall of a house. My left eye saw a woman with a pram approaching – one of my quirks is that I am a bit cockeyed, so I do have the ability to focus in two directions at once! What I saw made me almost miss the shot: peering out from behind the painted curtains was the tiny face of a child. You may have to look hard, but there it is: the twist of lemon!

Giant Rainbow Serpents moving through the sky, thirsty Water-holding
Frogs causing droughts, even elusive "bunyips" occupying Outback
billabongs – Aboriginal myth is unique in the many illustrative tales
of how the continent and its animals and seasons came to be. This
magnificent dreamtime-inspired mural of a serpent is in Bourke, a small
town on the Darling River in far-western New South Wales.

The world around us

The local primary school kids in Halls Creek, Western Australia, have given the town's rather drab old wheelie bins a vibrant facelift. The influence of Indigenous culture and the kids' connection with the world around them is immediately apparent.

Examples of mobile art (right) and not-so-mobile art (above and left) located in the historic town of Silverton, just outside Broken Hill, New South Wales.

IF IT MOVES, DRIVE IT: IF IT DOESN'T, PAINT IT!

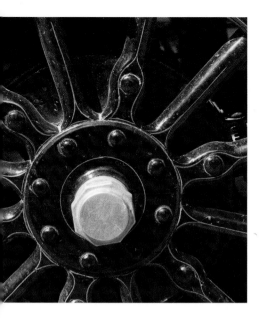

As a nation of four-wheel-drivers, Aussies often come back from long sojourns and view other folks as cityslickers. We wear an air of arrogance – we are the tough ones, the gladiatorial few who have the courage to venture Outback and beyond in our four-wheeled chariots.

Burke and Wills, Sturt, Blaxland, Leichhardt and all of the resourceful Aboriginal trackers before them must turn in their graves to see people cruising along in steel macho machines, complete with wide wheels, winches, fridges, airconditioning – not to mention GPS navigation! Just imagine being alone with the dust and the flies, lost in the wide open spaces with months of trekking behind you and God knows what else ahead. Macho? I don't think so. Not these days.

MACHO? I DON'T THINK SO!

Left: Remnants of a time before motorised transport, when men were men and wheels were often wooden.

Going ... Going ... **Ghan**

Opposite: Bill and Glenda relax in the afternoon light. **This page, clockwise from top left:** Oodnadatta's town sign in 1983; a poster from the old Ghan Railway; workers toiled for months in unbelievable heat to remove the old Ghan Railway.

Named after the Afghan camel drivers who opened up Central Australia, the old Ghan Railway likewise brought life and provisions to the South Australian Outback. A new Ghan Railway was built and re-routed through Tarcoola in 1980. Oodnadatta and other small towns on the now defunct route were confronted with big changes. Many people packed up and left, but Bill and Glenda (opposite) decided to build their corrugated iron and railway sleeper home on a dune many kilometres from the town. When asked how much the dwelling cost, Bill replied, "Well, the bulk of it is from the old Ghan, but I did spend one dollar – on roofing nails!"

The town of Peterborough in South Australia, like the UK town of the same name, is a railway town and a magnet for railway buffs. Situated on the junction of three different railway gauges, Peterborough is 253 kilometres north of Adelaide on the Barrier Highway. Each of the town's three entry points features authentic replicas of historical engines and carriages.

Overcoming scurvy

If you appreciate healthy eating and enjoy your meat and veggies fresh, then travelling in some areas of Australia without your own supplies can be a health hazard. Food-related quirk abounds in this country. Possibly the most famous of Australia's diners, where you don't have to worry about the meat, is Harry's Cafe de Wheels in Woolloomooloo, Sydney. Here the great Australian "pea floater" – a meat pie afloat in a sea of mushy peas – has reached gourmet levels.

Above left: Tongue-in-cheek meat marketing from Halls Creek in Western Australia. **Above right:** A sign speaks for itself in Yungaburra, north Queensland. **Opposite:** Harry's Cafe de Wheels, an elaborately decorated pie cart in Woolloomooloo, Sydney.

Above: A wall mural from the Oodnadatta Tuck Shop, South Australia.

Tucker time

On arriving in an outback town after a long, tiring drive, most people take their life in their hands and immediately begin trolling the streets for something resembling a take-away food outlet – commonly known as a "chew and spew". But that's assuming there is one and, if there is, that it's open! I patrolled Oodnadatta's main street on one such stomach-rumbling occasion and heaved a sigh of relief to see a sign reading "Tuck Shop". Closer inspection revealed another sign beneath the window that read, "Open every second Tuesday from 1 till 4 p.m."

Left: A ringer's tucker! This steak and marmalade sandwich was packed for me as lunch during a day with some ringers on Cape York in Queensland. When I opened it, I was unsure which was older: the sandwich or the newspaper it was wrapped in! Even the dogs treated this sanga with suspicion.

Loo art

There are few things as ugly as a concrete toilet block sitting in the middle of town. Even to contemplate entering some Australian dunnies is scary, but if you have a touch of outback tummy trouble after eating a steak and marmalade sanga, it might be unavoidable. Recently, however, there has been a movement (pardon the pun) in this country – art has come to the loo!

This art is not of the dunny-door poetry variety, but is usually themed to suit the character of the town in which it stands and is sometimes created in fastidious detail, as if vying for attention with other, more "traditional" attractions.

Above: A marine-themed loo at Wallaroo, a small town on the coast of the Yorke Peninsula in South Australia.

Loo art

Outback, Aboriginal and sea-themed
amenities from around Australia.

An **iron-clad** history...

Corrugated iron began appearing in Australia shortly after its invention in Britain in 1829, arriving along with other colonial exports of convicts, free settlers and supplies. During the 1850's gold rush hopeful fortune-seekers arrived carrying in their luggage portable dwellings numbered for assembly – the first corrugated-iron kit-homes! Also sent were shops, hotels, a theatre and three corrugated-iron churches. Now it has become such a part of Australian history that it is almost synonymous with outback architecture. Perhaps some still consider it the poor man's plaster, but today this versatile building material may be seen on even the finest, architect-designed Australian homes.

Right: A carefully painted historical mural from Outback Western Australia.
Above: Corrugated-iron detail from homesteads in Queensland.

An **iron-clad** history...

Above: Tropical motifs decorate a corrugated-iron dwelling in Queensland's Outback. **Right:** The "House of Wheels" in Winton, north-west Queensland.
Opposite top: Many corrugated-iron buildings are located in central Queensland.
Opposite bottom: A National Trust miner's house from the town of Ravenswood, central Queensland.

Above: The country is all about cars and cows, and these creative figures are among a great number of works that decorate a rural roadside property near Albany in Western Australia.
Opposite: In celebration of the legendary One-humped Camel of Norseman, Western Australia, these delightful works stand tall and proud in the centre of town.

Iron art

Corrugated-iron artwork may be found at some of the more prestigious art galleries in Australia, but stumbling across a piece of unexpectedly quirky iron art on one of Australia's bush properties is more rewarding.

A new era

Iron houses aren't the only architectural quirk from days gone by to be found in Australia. Dotted along the beaches of the Melbourne bayside suburbs of St Kilda and Brighton are small, brightly coloured bathing boxes, most of which were built in the mid-19th century but are now resplendent with contrasting colours and bright, beach-themed murals (these pages and pages 66–67).

It's the intrigue that's QUIRKY

The early 19th-century-built Port Pirie Railway Station (below) is one of Australia's brightest, most dramatic period buildings, but how was it perceived then? Few buildings please all of the people all of the time, and the intrigue that goes on behind the scenes gives the building a sense of humanity. In any case, the licence to create something different and avant-garde is quirky.

There must be a twinkle in an architect's eye when making the first pen stroke that will ultimately become an architectural wonder. Danish architect Jørn Utzon achieved fame when he designed the Sydney Opera House, but there were those who turned their noses up at the modern, creative structure at the time. Today it rivals Uluṟu as the most recognisable Australian icon.

Opposite: Port Pirie Railway Station (now a museum), South Australia. **Right:** The "milko" has delivered to the entrance of the Sydney Opera House, New South Wales.

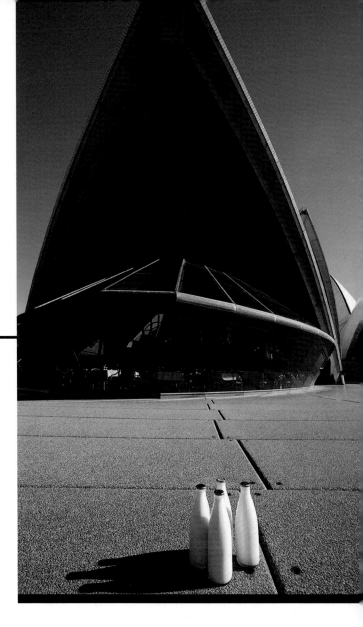

"Groovy for boarding, man!"

Perhaps the most recent and intense political backlash of modern Australian architecture was during the design and construction of Federation Square on the banks of the Yarra River in Melbourne. Many people adore the structure, particularly when twilight's colours play over the many textured panels; other people frown and concede that beauty truly is in the eye of the beholder. These three young Melburnians had only one reason to visit Federation Square – the surfaces are groovy for skateboarding!

Waste not, want not...

Architectural skills certainly aren't restricted to
the big city firms. Here at Lightning Ridge, an
opal-mining town in central New South Wales, locals
have constructed unique and comfortable homes
of eye-catching design. Mud brick, bottles, beer
cans, car doors for windows – someone has built
a home from it somewhere!

Winton's wall to beat all walls

Waste not want not

Outback Queensland boasts some truly stunning tourism sites, but this one near Winton isn't listed on the websites of the local tourist authorities. Known as "Arno's Wall", this fascinating piece of quirk is created from discarded objects, both old and modern, each meticulously placed and worked into the massive wall surrounding the artist's house.

Nick's revenge

Just after World War II, and having been deeply affected by his involvement in it, a young man named Nick Pecculas left Europe and settled in the small mining town of Sapphire, central Queensland. He purchased land adjacent to his mining lease and built a home there for himself and his wife. When his wife passed away, Nick constructed a "Pyramid of Peace" (left) in honour of her memory. To celebrate its construction, he wrote to the local shire inviting the council to use the pyramid for official functions. The council, however, would have none of it, which deeply offended Nick. He swore revenge.

Australians love a yarn about the "little man" who came off best against the bureaucrats, but unfortunately Nick's revenge was posthumously bittersweet. When he died Nick left the house and property to the council in his will, but because his house and the nearby Pyramid of Peace are built half on leasehold and half on land now belonging to the Department of Natural Resources, the council is unable to remove the structure, which is now preserved in all its glory.

Colckwise from above left: A colourful house at Cape Sorell, Macquarie Harbour, Tasmania; Willow Tree, the house of birds and flowers, New South Wales; house of weathervanes, north Queensland; house of swans, Jericho, central Queensland.

If you're proud of it, share it with the world!

Wagon wheels, fishing floats, painted stones, rubber-tyre swans, windmills – you name it, somebody collects it. Some collections grow so large that they fill the front, back and sides of the collector's dwelling. Some amuse and entertain crowds of passing tourists, others are so remote that they attract only passing crows, but the pleasure they provide for these delightful country "pack rats" is reason enough.

Collector's corner

Above and left: This multi-award-winning collection is from Coolgardie in the goldfields of Western Australia and represents a lifetime's work. The collection began indoors but the house became so full that the collector had to move his treasures into one of his own collectables – a small wooden caravan!

Collector's corner

Above: A collection near Port Fairy, Victoria.

Big is Beautiful

Australians have a fascination with anything larger than life – a big rock, a Great Barrier Reef – after all, it is a very big country! Anyone on a road trip of the continent is likely to encounter at least one of the nation's "big" objects, such as the Big Lobster at Kingston, South Australia. Huge amounts of seafood are consumed with gusto all along Australia's vast coastline, but at 17 metres high and weighing more than 4 tonnes, the Big Lobster would certainly fill a barbecue.

Left: The Big Lobster, a tourist attraction in Kingston, South Australia.

Clockwise from right: The Big Rocking Horse, Gumeracha, South Australia; Big Cane Toad, Sarina, Queensland; Big Pineapple, Nambour, Queensland; The Giant Ned Kelly, Glenrowan, Victoria; Big Barramundi, Daintree, North Queensland.
Pages 88–89: The Big Gumboot, Tully, Queensland.

The big buck spinner

Australia is home to the big banana, bushranger, rocking horse, prawn, sheep, Galah, mosquito, pineapple, golden guitar, cow, macadamia nut, crab, Tasmanian Devil, crocodile, Cane Toad, wine cask, oyster, potato – even a big dunny was considered! This love affair with large has been part of Aussie culture for a long time. It's all just a bit of fun, but in some towns there is actually little else to keep the cash flowing in and few tourists can resist a souvenir. Every icon has a story, some connected to history, others representative of local produce or regional events. The Big Gumboot, in Tully (pages 88–89), is an annual event and the gumboot itself is an award celebrating the high rainfall of the district.

Big is Beautiful

Big is Beautiful

Wagin, 229 kilometres south of Perth, is serious sheep country, which becomes obvious the moment you drive into this quaint, rural town that has buildings decorated with murals of sheep. In early March Wagin's annual "Woolarama" celebrates the woolly wanderers' contribution to the nation's prosperity. It is the biggest sheep show in Western Australia and attracts up to 25,000 people from throughout the land.

There are several Big Rams around Australia, but the one at Wagin stands 7 metres tall and 15 metres long and, according to the locals, is definitely the biggest. Of course, one would never dispute this while propping up the bar with a bunch of blokes whose muscles hint at decades of shearing and working the land!

Mine is **bigger** than yours!

When I happened across the unique shepherd's wagon (left), it was as though I had slipped back through time to the turn of the century when wagons like this one were commonplace on outback roads. But would the guys drinking tin mugs of tea allow me to photograph them? I plucked up the courage to ask and boldly approached them, saying, "Hi, I'm doing a book on the Great Dividing Range..." There was a pregnant pause. Neither man looked up. Then the oldest, obviously the man in charge, without even lifting his mouth from his mug, said, "Solongaswedon'thave tatalktoya!" That was the shortest, most eloquent approval I have had in 30 years of photographing Australians.

The LONG PADDOCK

Australia's national dictionary, the Macquarie, defines "long paddock" as "a stock route or open road, especially regarded as a place where people, too poor to own their own paddocks or pay for agistment, can graze their horses, cattle, etc". These stock routes are very important in Australia, the driest inhabited continent, especially when the land is parched by drought. The nation's climate is one of extreme variability, and while farmers have worked out how to make a living for the benefit of the nation, there is a problem associated with that: land degradation from the constant tramping of stock.

Above, clockwise from top left: The late Iris Buntine, Australia's longest-serving outback telephonist, from Stonehenge, Queensland; Gwyneth and Bill Ostling, outback preachers from the Church of the Catacombs, an underground church at Coober Pedy, South Australia; smiling kids say "cheese" for a photo at Morgan State School, South Australia. **Opposite:** A mob of Aussies in Brisbane, Queensland.

94

We're a **weird** mob...

What a dull world it would be if we weren't each just a little quirky in our own way!

Above: Perhaps too many sunsets influenced the colour of this buffalo outside Darwin, Northern Territory. **Right:** The cool of sunset provides a brief respite during the Silly Season. **Opposite:** A local artist proudly displays his impressions of a tropical sunset.

For those Aussies who live in the continent's sweltering Tropical North, or even those visiting for a prolonged period, "Going troppo" (becoming disturbed) is considered a seasonal phenomenon. Depending on the weather, the "Silly Season" runs between December and February, when even those born and bred in the tropics struggle with the heat and humidity. As the mercury rises to well over 35° Celsius and the humidity becomes stifling, silly behavior may also occur by degrees. To avoid the heat-induced madness, seasoned Darwinites migrate from their homes in the early evening, taking with them a hamper, bottle of wine, folding card table and collapsible chairs. They perch themselves on the western cliff tops of Fannie Bay, refreshing their overheated bodies in the cool sea breeze, and there, with few words exchanged, they gaze out across the Timor Sea, tinged by the beauty of a fading pink sky.

When Darwinites come together for a celebration there is always a riot of colour.

Above: The Grand Parade during the Festival of Darwin.
Left and top right: The Variety Club Bash at Mindil Beach. **Right:** Brightly coloured bicycles adorn a float in the festival.

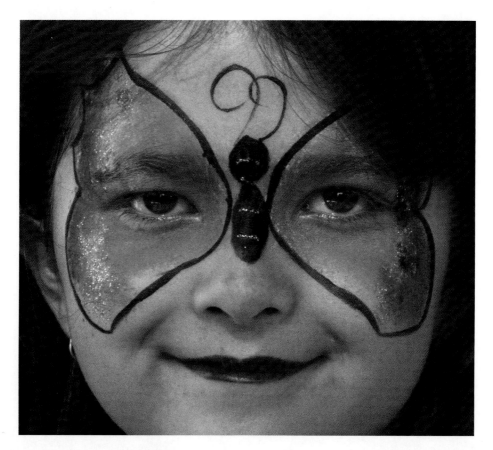

The face of a nation?

When it comes to the human face, quirk reigns supreme, especially when a little creative ingenuity is applied.

Above: Face painting at a street fair in Darwin, Northern Territory. **Opposite:** A highly painted performer at the opening of Federation Square in Melbourne, Victoria.

Mad hatters...

Melbourne Cup Day in November, the horse race that stops a nation, is the best time to see eccentric millinery – nearly every woman wears a fabulously over-the-top hat. But you may feel the need to take your hat off to some of the everyday headgear you spot as well, whether a tattered, old outback Akubra™ or something more exotic!

Above: A Tasmanian Devil hat from Hobart in Tasmania.

Opposite: A feather collection from Goulburn in New South Wales.

Every shoe has a story

Footwear, in the right time and place – or somewhere you least expect to find it! – can be intriguing. Who owned and abandoned it, and why? Thongs are the favoured footwear for many Aussies, especially near the beaches, but most people in the Outback find that they can't put a foot wrong with a tough, nicely worn-in pair of workboots.

Above left: Twisted by time, this goldminer's boot was found near a discarded mine site on Western Australia's goldfields. **Above right:** A young Aboriginal boy from Coen on Cape York Peninsula wears these boots with pride. **Left:** Even with the rocky terrain, thongs are the preferred footwear for this Aboriginal man who is grinding ochre to make paint for cave painting.

Above: Those visiting the islands off Queensland's Great Barrier Reef need protective shoes in order to wander across the coral flats without damaging the reef or their feet. What great stories these shoes could tell of the reef's hidden secrets, the creatures and corals crushed underfoot – if only they had real tongues instead of synthetic ones!

Australia's ankle biters...

Sometimes it's the things kids do, other times it's what they say, but they sure know how to raise a laugh.

Opposite top left: This wall painting expresses the exuberant optimism of kids. **Left to right:** Playing on a swing in Alice Springs, Northern Territory; Aboriginal children from Kalumburu in the Kimberley try out an innovative method of bush transport; When I asked this young fellow why he wasn't in school on a Wednesday morning at 10 a.m., his reply was instantaneous, "Cause yer don't get paid for doin' that do yer?"

Characters carved in stone

Just up the Innamincka Road from the historic railway town of Lyndhurst, South Australia, is the home and gallery of one of Down Under's true characters, locally known as "Talc Alf". For over 30 years, the Dutch-born, Australian-raised Cornelius Alferink has been carving out his niche in Australian tourism, both with his unusual and beautiful talc sculptures of places, people and events and his eccentric explanation of the origins of the alphabet. Alf is artist, poet and philosopher all in one quirky package.

Boxing kangaroos

Above: Fred (far right) with wife Josie and the kids (left) and their team of fighters.
Opposite, clockwise from top: Folks fly in from miles around for the big day of the Birdsville Races; the Birdsville pub at sunrise before the rush; race day drinkers overflow from inside the bustling Birdsville Hotel.

Ask Fred Brophy – famous for his boxing troupe, which any hard, back-country man brave enough or stupid enough can challenge to win a buck or two – what life is like as a professional outback boxing troupe manager and his reply is classic:

"When things are bad, which is most of the time, it's roo steaks and billabong water.

When things are sort of OK, it's beer and meat pies.

When things are bloody fabulous, which they always are at Birdsville around race day, then it's caviar and champagne!"

Letterbox wars!

Once upon a time, on a lonely country road in Tasmania, a farmer decided to "tart up" his letterbox and create something special that the whole community could appreciate. As time passed, each member of the small rural community, not wanting to be upstaged, decided that they too would create their very own special letterbox. Soon every farm but one had constructed a stunning letterbox and all who passed by slowed down to admire the handiwork. It was some weeks before the final farm decided to erect a letterbox. When it did, the community was shocked. There, stuck at the top of a pole, was an old, cracked plastic can beneath which hung a sign: "Youse can all piss off, then!"

Once upon a time, on a lonely country road in Tasmania…

Left: "Hughie" the *Muttaburrasaurus*, at Hughenden. **Right:** Kronosaurus Korner, at Richmond, features more than 200 exhibits of fossilised remains from Australia's Cretaceous inland sea. It includes the Richmond Marine Fossil Museum (with laboratory) and employs a qualified palaeontologist-curator and two centre assistants full-time. As well as being a popular tourist attraction, Kronosaurus Korner provides research opportunities for palaeontology students.

STEP BACK IN TIME

If you were to drive west across the Overlander Highway in the dead of night and round the corner into the town of Hughenden, your headlights would illuminate a 14-metre-high dinosaur! Hughenden is located at the easternmost point of Queensland's famous fossil triangle and bills itself, unashamedly, as *Muttaburrasaurus* territory. A replica of the plant-eating *Muttaburrasaurus*, which roamed central north Queensland more than 100 million years ago, is the centrepiece of the town's dinosaur museum. "Hughie'", as he is known, was modelled from the first entire fossil skeleton found in Australia.

Expect the
unexpected

Mannequins are often used to attract attention and the quirkier they are the better but, *Muttaburrasaurus* aside, they are the last thing one would expect to find in a dry and dusty outback town. Mount Surprise in north Queensland, however, certainly lives up to its name with these lifelike ladies (left).

The more stylised figures (right) enjoy an elevated status in the city as a café owner in Acland Street, Melbourne, attempts to outdo the competition.

Tourists flock from around the world to watch the sun sink below the imposing crimson rock of Uluru.

A religious experience

Indigenous Australians have been aware of the awesome spiritual power of Uluru for centuries.
Now everyone is catching on to the raw red beauty of this magical place. Sunset viewing at Uluru
is the single most sought-after experience in Australia. Tourists flock from around the world to
spend the last few hours of a Northern Territory evening waiting for the sun to set, anticipating the
rock turning picture-postcard crimson. The car park seen opposite is one venue; another, further
back in the dunes, is for tourist buses. Here, tour guides arrive early to lay out tables covered with
white tablecloths, canapés and rows of wine glasses. It is a mesmerising experience just to sit,
watch and listen. Many first-timers are overcome with emotion and burst into a sudden flood of
tears. For me, the rock is a classic piece of Aussie quirk: remote, exposed and weathered, baking
in the hot Australian sun.

Heart-stopping landscape

Whether for Australians on their first trip around their nation or for international visitors used to vastly different countryside, Australia's scenic beauty, stark landscapes and associated flora can be simply stunning. Many of Australia's rugged attractions are iconic, attracting millions of visitors annually. However, even a strangely formed gum tree or a giant Boab within close proximity of a highway or a road less travelled, often reveals a well-worn walking track.

Above: River Red Gum,
Flinders Ranges National Park, South Australia.
Right: A Boab from the Kimberley,
Western Australia.

Heart-stopping landscape

Left to right: Three very special Australian landscapes –
the Three Sisters, Blue Mountains, New South Wales; the Pinnacles, Nambung
National Park, Western Australia; the Twelve Apostles, Port Campbell National
Park, Victoria. **Opposite, inset:** One of the limestone stacks of the Twelve
Apostles recently toppled into the ocean.

Before **After**

Australia's landscapes are punctuated with dramatic monoliths, but visitors to some of them may get more – or less! – than they bargained for. Sightseers at the Twelve Apostles recently saw one of the pillars crumble into the ocean. But don't wait for them to be renamed the Eleven Apostles – there were only ever nine orginally!

NO.

NO DOGS (UNDER THE AGE OF 18 YEARS) ALLOWED

TRESPASSERS will be executed

NOTICE
INSURANCE AGENTS
CAR SALES MEN
JEHOVAN'S WITNESSES
YOU ARE NOT
WELCOME

NO WHERE ELSE

A sign of the times

Signs – some of which I am
sure are are not intended to be
amusing, such as the threat to
execute – often provide some
cheeky fun for tourists and
photographers.

One sign on the Eyre Peninsula
simply read "Nowhere". I drove one
hundred kilometres out of my way
just for a photograph to find that
the sign had been stolen. I was
consoled only when I discovered the
sign shown opposite (bottom right),
in Tasmania. Mad, eccentric and
quirky as this continent is, I wouldn't
have it any other way, because it is
true – Australia certainly is like "No
Where Else".

Index

BRADT TRAVEL GUIDES
www.bradtguides.com

online

FOR PRODUCTS
www.steveparish.com.au

FOR LIMITED EDITION PRINTS
www.steveparishexhibits.com.au

FOR PHOTOGRAPHY EZINE
www.photographaustralia.com.au

© Copyright 2008 Steve Parish Publishing Pty Ltd
This edition published in the UK by Bradt Travel Guides Ltd
23 High Street, Chalfont St Peter, Bucks SL9 9QE, England
Published in the USA by The Globe Pequot Press Inc
246 Goose Lane, PO Box 480, Guilford, Connecticut 06475-0480

Steve Parish Publishing Pty Ltd
PO Box 1058,
Archerfield,
Queensland 4108
Australia

British Library Cataloguing in Publication Data
A catalogue record for this book is available from the British Library
ISBN-10: 1 84162 237 0
ISBN-13:   978 1 84162 237 8

Photography: Steve Parish
Additional photography:
Cover and pp. 28–9, sculptures by Jan Mitchell, Baywalk Bollards;
p. 18 Ian Morris; p. 19 Pat Slater; p. 25 bottom, Pat Slater; pp. 33 mural by John Lendis;
p. 82 Ian Morris; p. 123 bottom, Glen Watson, courtesy of Warrnambool Standard.

Text: Steve Parish

Design: Gill Stack, SPP

Editorial: Karin Cox, SPP

Acknowledgements:
The publishers are grateful for permission to reproduce copyright material. While every effort has been
made to trace copyright holders, the publishers would be pleased to hear from any not acknowledged.

Prepress by Colour Chiefs Digital Imaging, Australia

Produced in Australia at the Steve Parish Publishing Studios

Printed and bound in India at Nutech Photolithographers